HOW TO *WRITE* A BOOK

KYLE SEARCY

Unless otherwise indicated, all scripture quotations are taken from the New *King James Bible*.

Counterintuitive Leadership
ISBN 978-1-64764-051-4
Copyright 2020
Kyle Searcy

Published by
KCS Leadership Institute
Montgomery, AL 36116
334-613-3363

Printed in the United States of America.
All rights reserved under International Copyright Law. Contents and/or cover may not be reproduced in whole or in part in any form without written consent of the Publisher.

HOW TO
WRITE
A BOOK

CONTENTS

Introduction 1
Chapter 1 – Figure Out 5
Chapter 2 – Map Out 11
Chapter 3 – Write Out 23
Chapter 4 – Illustrate 35
Chapter 5 – Transition 39
Chapter 6 – Edit 43
Chapter 7 – Typeset 49
Chapter 8 – Print 53
Chapter 9 – How To Market Your Book 57
Conclusion 67

INTRODUCTION

I was walking through the Atlanta airport feeling not so great about life. I hate to admit it, but I was having a one-man pity party. Although I am usually pretty positive, that day I felt inept. It was many years ago, but I remember it vividly. As I walked to the gate for my next flight, I rehearsed several things that hadn't gone right for the last few months…

"You idiot! Why did you do that?"

"You could have been further along if you hadn't made that stupid decision."

I was beating myself up pretty badly. Have you ever had one of those whinny days? They're pretty miserable. I had earned a PhD in "whine-ology" that day.

I kept walking, pondering my incompetence, when I noticed a bookstand. I drew near and saw two books by fellow Pastors.

"What are these books doing in the airport? This is not a Christian Bookstore!"

One book was by T.D. Jakes, the famous Pastor of the Potter's House in Dallas, Texas and the other book was by Rod Parsley, the Senior Pastor of World Harvest Church in Columbus, Ohio. When I saw those books, envy knocked on my heart, and I opened the door. That envy intensified my personal verbal flogging.

"God look at that! You have never done anything like this for me! These guys' books are everywhere!" Just as I was sucking my teeth in disappointment, God **spoke** to me. He really did! It wasn't a loud, booming voice in a British accent, like in the movies, but in my heart and mind I clearly heard Him.

"Son, they *wrote* the books!"

The words were corrective but there was love connected to it somehow. I was able to hear it and reason again.

I realized I had never finished any of the books I started writing. How was God going to open doors for books *I had **not** written* to be promoted and sold?

That cured my pity. I went home and started writing. It wasn't easy, but I got my first book, *The Power of Passion* done. Shortly after that book, my second one was finished. Then the third, fourth, fifth, and sixth books all saw the light of day. I kept on writing until something special happened with my tenth book.

I was walking in Wal-Mart one day, shopping cart full of items, and I stepped over to the bookrack. As I looked over the books, I spotted it! There were several copies of my 10th book, *The Secrets of Biblical Wisdom*! I couldn't believe it. It wasn't the Atlanta airport, but it was good enough for me.

This reminded me of a valuable truth we need to remind ourselves of. Here it is…are you ready for it?

A BOOK NEVER WRITTEN NEVER GETS READ.

I want to help you write your book.

It isn't uncommon for a lot of people to consider writing as a Herculean task that involves being a recluse and surrounded by heaps and heaps of books and lots and lots of coffee. However, it isn't a true assessment of writing or writers, and it's one of the reasons why a lot of people consider writing a book an ambition that is too lofty for them.

Let me break it down for you.

A lot of people aren't aware of the truth, and the truth is that writing a book is not as daunting as many people think. In fact, with the right mindset, you can start and complete your book in less time than you think. Yes, You.

I've had interactions with many people who have expressed a burning desire to write a book, but they don't think they have the talent to do it. While talent is an important factor for becoming a successful author – especially in fiction and poetry – it isn't a requirement for writing a good book. In reality, we're all talented writers in varying degrees. We are all capable of writing. We've been writing since our formative years.

A book never written never gets read.

Similarly, no one goes through college without having to write something. The reason why a lot of people think they can't write is because they have created a mental block for themselves. The mental block is usually caused by the mystery that writing has always been shrouded in. In this book, I will demystify this mental block and put you through the process of writing your first book.

To put it simply, the belief that writing is hard is a myth. In most cases, the problem isn't writing down your thoughts or the knowledge you have, the problem is organizing the work, structuring your thoughts and putting a coherent work together. In this book, you will learn how to structure your thoughts and organize the things you want to say. If you've always thought that the precious ideas you have will never be shared with the world because you lack the talent to write a good book, it's time to change your mind. I'll put you on the path to starting and completing your first book. Your dream of becoming an author is about to be fulfilled.

Before you start writing anything, you need to know what you want to say. This book will teach you how to put those ideas together to form a good book. If you don't have anything to say, you will need to take a step back and work on that first.

If you don't believe you can do it, you'll never get it done.

Writing isn't for everybody. Some communicate better through visual images, or movement, or through data and numbers. But for those who are willing to embrace words, writing can be an exciting journey!

The first thing you need to know is that **YOU CAN WRITE A BOOK!** In fact, this should be the only thing in your mind. Writing is like any other challenge -- if you don't believe you can do it, you'll never get it done. The most important work you will need to do is to adopt the mindset of a winner. I'd be deceiving you if I told you that writing is easy. It isn't. You will need to be very motivated to start a writing project and complete it. This shouldn't scare you, however. Nothing worthwhile comes easily. You have to work hard for anything you truly want.

The journey to writing your first book begins here…

ONE

FIGURE OUT

I'VE BEEN KNOWN TO be spontaneous. Sometimes I want to go with the flow of life, and that's exactly what I did for vacation one year. My wife and I were tired and needed a getaway, so I asked my wife Kemi to pack a bag for a 3-day excursion.

"Where are we going?"

"You will see."

"What kind of clothes do I pack? "

"Just normal clothes. Nothing dressy."

"Ok."

We got in the car and started driving. The truth is I had no plan. After driving for about 30 minutes she asked again, "Where are we going?"

"This way," I said, pointing ahead with a confident smile.

We just kept driving, talking and enjoying each other. After four and a half hours we found ourselves in Nashville, Tennessee. I pulled up to the Grand Ole Opry House to see if my Marriott discount would be honored. They accepted it giving us access to an inexpensive hotel room in a gorgeous environment.

That was the *only* positive thing that happened on the vacation. The shows we wanted to see were sold out, or the ticket lines were too long. The only available shows were of no interest to us. We basically stayed in a hotel room for three days then drove back home. Our vacation would have been so much better if I simply took the time to develop a plan before leaving.

Don't approach book writing the same way I started my trip -- without thought or plan. This way is not ideal.

THE MAP

Writing a book takes time – especially if it's your first time. It can take weeks or months of concerted effort. You don't have to spend years to write, but you do need a structure and a plan. This is usually the point where a lot of people miss it, they think writing is a thing that you just sit down to do without mapping out your every step.

The significance of planning isn't just because it will help in writing from start to finish and prevent you from going off-topic. A plan will help you to easily get back on track. It will also prevent you from running out of ideas or having ideas which haven't been thought through well enough.

Before starting to write, you may feel you know it all, but the truth is, the moment you start writing, you may go blank. When you have an overall plan, your focus is more directed. You know what is in the chapter you are working on, and what is in the next chapter. You can concentrate on making your thoughts and ideas clear for your reader.

A solid plan will help you organize your work effectively. Have you ever read a book and you feel the work doesn't just come together as well as it should? That's because the work probably wasn't properly organized. The foundation for a book that is well-organized is proper planning.

Step 1
What is your subject?

The first thing you need to do is to figure out what you want to write about. Let's look at the subject of love. It's huge. Do you want to write about romantic relationships? The love of God? The love of family? Love of friends? Love for career? How to love yourself better? In the process of planning your book, whittle down your idea to the most important thing you want to talk about and build the entire book around it.

This phase is called "figure out" because it is the phase where you get to see how solid your idea is. Book ideas, in most cases, come in a vague form, you have to refine them before they can become something you can work with. In the process of refining, some ideas are going to be too weak to write a book about. If you jump into writing a book based on the initial idea that you get, you may soon find yourself out of ideas.

> *The first thing you need to do is to figure out what you want to write about.*

THE PROPOSAL

One of the best ways to refine your idea and whittle it down to the most important elements is by writing a proposal. Writing a proposal is not compulsory in every case, but it is recommended. If you're planning to self-publish, you don't have to write a proposal, but I recommend that you do write one. You will definitely have to write a proposal if you're trying to get publishers to publish your book. But no matter which path (self-publishing or traditional publisher), a proposal is a very good way to think long and hard about what you want to say and why you are the one to say it.

The goal of a book proposal is to convince a publisher that your idea is good and that they should invest in it. Writing a proposal will force you to look at your idea, look at the market for other books like yours, and show how your book can be profitable. Even if you self-publish, this is a beneficial use of your time. It gives you valuable information about important issues concerning your idea and its marketability. After all, once you write your book, you want others to purchase it, right? Publishers are all about business, so you need a very solid idea, and you need to be very convincing to get them to accept your proposal. If you find it difficult to come up with a proposal for your book, it probably means that the idea needs more work.

> *The goal of a book proposal is to convince a publisher that your idea is good and that they should invest in it.*

An interested publisher wants to see a book proposal, rather than the final book. A successful proposal has to be thoroughly researched, clearly presented, and persuasive. It is usually a manuscript of about 15-50 pages and is meant to capture the entire message of the book succinctly. A good proposal must include what the book is about, how the message will be conveyed, why you believe you're in the best position to write it, and the market to whom the book will appeal.

Being able to write a good proposal is the first step towards being able to write a good book. While some people choose to write the proposal after completing the book, it is advisable for you to write yours before you start writing the book. By the time you finish your book proposal, you would have successfully refined your idea into something you can write extensively about and conquered some of the things that seemed too scary for you to attempt earlier.

You can write the proposal yourself or opt for some help. A professional editor can help you refine and edit your proposal, or you can hire a professional ghostwriter to write the entire proposal from start to finish.

For those who need some more guidance with writing a book proposal, there are many good templates available online. Here are some links to websites with good templates:

https://scribewriting.com/book-proposal-template/

https://blog.reedsy.com/how-to-write-a-book-proposal/

https://www.tckpublishing.com/wp-content/uploads/2018/08/Book-Proposal-Template.docx

https://www.tckpublishing.com/wp-content/uploads/2019/08/Book-Proposal-Sample.pdf

https://www.pandadoc.com/book-proposal-template/

https://www.template.net/business/proposal-templates/book-proposal-template/

Once you have figured out what you are going to talk about, you will need to flesh out the structure of the book. Let explore how this is done.

TWO

MAP OUT

I LOVE GPS. WHOEVER CAME up with the idea should be in a Hall of Fame somewhere. I seldom take note of streets or landmarks anymore. Why should I? There are satellites hovering above the earth that constantly track my position and give me profound situational awareness. The awareness comes when my position is plotted on a map. This positioning allows me to see exactly where I am and determine precisely where I want to go. Mapping out your book before you start writing will work just like a global positioning system as you write your book. It will help you know where you are, and where you are going.

Irrespective of the genre of the book you're writing, mapping out a strategy for the book is very important – the only exemption from this may be poetry. Even with poetry, the book will have some kind of theme or structure, as determined by the poems selected. In writing fiction or nonfiction, mapping out the book is crucial. Imagine you are in the woods, and you start walking, taken in by the beauty of the forest. After a couple of hours, you want to turn back, but you have no compass. You have no map.

You don't have breadcrumbs to follow. You are lost. Writing without a map can be like this. In our forest analogy, the logical thing to do is to create a marker or reminder of some sort at every turn to be reminded of where to turn on the way back.

For those uninspired by nature, consider shopping. Have you ever gone to the store without a shopping list? Did you buy unnecessary things or forget the things you needed? When you write without an outline, you are most likely going to forget some of the things that you should talk about in the book.

The first thing to do when mapping out is to think about your idea and how it is organized. For example, if I wanted to write a book about American Barbecue, I might decide to talk about:

- the history of barbecue,
- types of meats used in barbecue,
- the type of wood/best smoke to use depending on your goal,
- the general procedures for cooking barbecue,
- regional specialties/sauces (Carolina, Memphis, Texas, Kansas City, etc.)
- award winning barbecue chefs
- barbecue recipes
- barbecue restaurants, etc.

This book would be at least 10 chapters, probably more, as barbecue is a broad subject. You can see a logical order from history to meats – smoke – procedure for cooking – sauces – recipes – restaurants. Another writer may place the chapters in a different order, and that's ok. You decide what your focus is and outline it. The outline keeps you focused and on task.

The next thing is to choose titles for these chapters. Having a chapter title is not necessary for fiction or creative nonfiction writers, however, it is important for anyone writing any other type of nonfiction to create chapter titles. It gives you a starting point. Then, you create an outline for each chapter. In our fictional barbecue book, the chapter on sauces may start with the supermarket sauces we know, and how they do not represent true barbecue culture. Each region has specialty sauces. Then you may want to talk about the Carolina vinegar/mustard sauce, or dry rub/no sauce, or Kansas City and the tomato-based sauce, or Alabama white sauce or any of the other variants from other regions. The outline and title you create for each chapter can be tweaked as you progress, because ideas change. I know that outlining the book and the chapters sounds like a lot of work before you even start writing, but it will make the actual writing process go much faster once you have done the mapping out in the beginning.

Another purpose of mapping out is to allow you the freedom to write without having to bother yourself with what to write about at each turn. If you fail to create an outline and title for each chapter before you begin, you will have to divide your time between writing and thinking of what to write about when you finally start to write. Each new chapter will present the challenge of what to talk about, how to talk about it, and the number of words to create. That is a challenge that could have been avoided if the outline was created for each chapter right from the beginning.

While some writers may find it easier to write without an outline, it isn't advisable for someone writing their first book.

In creating chapters and titles, it is important to arrange them in a logical order. It would make it a grueling process for the readers to go through if each chapter is structurally disconnected from the previous one. Your work is to arrange the chapters in such a way that it would be easy for the readers to follow from chapter to chapter. Logical and structural arrangement of chapters is very important in writing a book. For instance, it would be difficult for the readers to follow if the first chapter of a book about driving a car talks about how to open the door, then the next chapter talks about how to make a turn, and the chapter after that talks about putting the key into the ignition. Readers will find themselves constantly lost and having to track back if the chapters are not arranged logically. The expectation may be a little different for fiction and creative nonfiction writers, they have more freedom in this aspect. They can deliberately jump a scene to create suspense without losing the readers in anyway. However, nonfiction writers do not enjoy similar liberty.

Beyond having chapter titles and outlines, it's important that you have a projected word count that you believe will be enough to capture your ideas. This is another part of your map – as you go, things change, but it's good to have a goal. All these may sound unnecessary at the beginning, but as you progress in writing your own book, it becomes entirely different. The word count goal for your book may not be an easy decision for you to make. There are many factors that will determine the number of words you are going to settle with. Your subject, your audience and your writing ability will influence your word count.

- 10,000 words – this is similar to a pamphlet or business white paper; it takes about two hours – or less – for a fast reader to consume it. Anyone can finish it in a few hours. It is perfect if you're trying to create useful tips for people to read quickly or have a subject that can be covered in a few words. This style is also a good supplement to social media, where long form writing isn't done.
- 20,000 words – this is a short eBook. It is more engaging than 10,000 words and it is perfect if you're trying to create a book that can be read quickly, but you want to include more details than what 10,000 can afford to give you. For a fast reader, such a document would take about four to five hours to read, it may take a lot more for a slow reader.
- 40,000 – 60,000 words – this is the word count for a standard nonfiction book/novella; it is not very thick if printed out, and it can be used to convey a very big topic. It may take days for a reader to finish this book, depending on the speed of the reader.
- 80,000 – 100,000 words – this is a very long book; it could be fiction or nonfiction. A lot of novels fall under this category, it is the standard word count for a lot of adventure and historical novels. This type of book takes

a longer time to read. Serious dedication and consistency would be needed to complete the manuscript for this kind of book.

100,000+ words – there's no limit for the number of words you can have in a single book, there have been books with over 500,000 words. The important thing here is to consider your audience and what they'd be interested in.

While you can write as many words as you feel like writing, it is not advisable to write something that is too lengthy for your first book. There are certain rules guiding the number of words you can adopt to tell a story or talk about an idea. These rules are not set in stone. Writers like JRR Tolkien, who are famous for writing books of extreme lengths, started out writing books that fit the accepted word count of their genre. They built a big audience for their work before they started to move out of the convention. Choosing to go to extreme word counts for your first book may make it unappealing for your target audience.

To conclude this section, it is important to emphasize that the biggest mistake you'll make as someone writing their first book is not to map out or create an outline. In fact, I believe it is one of the main reasons why a lot of people never complete their books -- because they started without a plan. Creating an outline will be easier if you take the time to properly work on your idea before you start writing.

COMING UP WITH A GREAT BOOK TITLE

Writing a book title is one of the most challenging things for a writer. The book title is the first thing that attracts the reader or make them disinterested. Forget about how good your content is. No one will pick the book up to check the content if the title isn't great. A lot of people don't realize it until they are about to title their own book but titling a book can be very tricky. Everyone wants a title that is catchy and meaningful, a title that will make anyone that sees the book want to pick it up. A good title should convey the central theme of the book without giving away the ending. It shouldn't be too long or too short. Not many people are going to be interested in reading a book that has the same title has many other books out there. For many writers, the task of coming up with a title is more stressful than any other thing they have to do. The title is a few words that have to sound right. There is no shortcut to getting a good title. You may be lucky to come up with a great title easily, but many writers aren't always that lucky. Here are a few tips that can help you in coming up with great titles:

Finish first

Titling your book shouldn't be your first priority. In fact, it shouldn't be your priority at all until you finish the book. This doesn't mean that you should ignore it when you get a good idea for a book title, but if in the process of writing, a good idea for the book title strikes you, write it down somewhere and continue your work. A time is coming that coming up with a book title will be the most important thing, but at the beginning, writing and finishing up should be the most important. You can come up with a "working title" at the beginning, but it is usually a rough draft of the title, something that is temporary and most definitely going to change. The truth is, after writing the book you will start to get a clearer picture of what the title could be.

Don't over-promise

Many people make the mistake of trying to make the book so catchy that they go overboard and over-promise. Over-promising is not so different from clickbait. It draws readers in with a catchy title, but the content is lean. Over-promising may get a few people to buy your first book, but your book will not get good reviews and it will affect how your subsequent books are received. Words like "Revolutionary," "Epic," "Guaranteed," etc., should be avoided. It would be disappointing if people buy a book titled, "Revolutionary Ways to Change Your Life," and there's nothing revolutionary or life-changing about it. I won't tell you to under-promise, but it's better if readers and critics give your book such praise in their reviews. Buyers hate to be lied to. Readers are buyers who invest their money and time on your product, so be fair to them.

Try to make it short, but don't be afraid of long titles

Short titles are very good. Consider a book like *Becoming* by Michelle Obama. It's catchy, effective, and lets you know she is writing about how she came to be. Michelle Obama could have gotten away with any title, because she is an instantly recognizable person. Popular writers like Stephen King or Nora Roberts can get away with any title. Titles that people can read at a glance are excellent. Another advantage of short titles is that they can be easily remembered and recommended. For instance, it's easier to ask, "Have you read *Rich Dad, Poor Dad*?" than to say, "You should read *The Adventures of a Rich Dad and the Misadventures of a Poor Dad*?" If your title isn't short, make sure it is appropriate for your subject and you have a reason to justify its length.

Consider subtitles

The use of subtitles is quite popular in nonfiction books, and it's something you can consider for your book as well. Subtitle is a great way to clarify the desired outcome from reading the book. Usually, there's a part of the title that is short and catchy, which is usually used to lure the readers, while the subtitle does the work of clarifying what readers will get from the book. Before creating a subtitle, you have to consider how your subtitle can further expand achieving certain outcomes, the biggest problems that your subtitle can provide solutions for, and many more. Some examples of good use of subtitles are, *Roots: The Saga of an American Family* by Alex Haley; *Peter Pan: The Boy Who Wouldn't Grow Up* by James Matthew Barrie; *Instinct: The Power to Unleash Your God Given Drive* by T.D. Jakes; etc. It's possible to use subtitles in some books of fiction as well, especially to help differentiate the novels in a series.

Subtitles are very good because they allow you the liberty to say more than a regular title would afford you. Nobody wants to pick up a book with an unnecessarily long title; however, with the use of subtitles the length of the title becomes more acceptable.

Avoid clichés

Self-help and motivational books are quite popular, and it is very easy to join the bandwagon of writing about how to make millions in half a minute. The fact that everyone is trying to get the attention of the readers means that almost everyone is working around the same cliché title. A lot of readers scoff when they see these cliché titles, try to avoid them as much as possible. Cliché titles are quite popular in fiction too, with too many people talking about "the adventures" of this or "the tales" of that. Try to go for more creative and original titles.

List your favorite lines

An easy way to come up with a good book title is to write down the phrases you like the most from the book. These phrases may not automatically work as book titles, but they can give you the idea to play around. There are titles that are direct phrases from the book, and there are titles that draw inspiration from related quotes. For instance, the title of the book *Things* Fall Apart by Chinua Achebe was drawn from the poem "Second Coming" by W.B Yeats.

Draw inspiration from other titles

One thing about good titles is that they spark inspiration for other good titles. You can look at other book titles in a similar genre as yours and try to draw inspiration from them. While it is hard to charge another author for plagiarizing a title, it is not advisable to copy someone else's title anyway. Look at the titles you like, identify the things that appeal to you in those titles and use them as a template to brainstorm for your own title.

Go for titles that are unforgettable

The best trick is to aim at making the best impression from the beginning. Make the title catchy and memorable. Consider titles like, "I'm Lying but I'm Saying the Truth," "Trust me, I'm Lying: Confessions of a Media Manipulator," etc. There are many titles that make use of alliteration to make the title easier to read and remember. Make the title clever and interesting.

Generating title ideas for fiction and nonfiction may involve looking at different places and considering different factors. The genre will determine the kind of book title that will be deemed appropriate. Draw up different titles, maybe as many as twenty, and then gradually start to narrow them down. Choosing the appropriate title may take you a while, so don't rush it. Examine each title and critique each one. Read the titles out loud and put yourself in the position of the buyer, would you be tempted to pick the book up with any of the titles you have already? Another thing is to ask for the opinion of others. Ask your family and friends the title that is most likely to convince them to buy the book if they were strangers. Sometimes, our individual bias and attachment may cloud our sense of judgement, but with the feedback of others, you will be able to come to a better conclusion. Just like it is with writer's block, if you feel like the ideas aren't coming together as they should for the title, you can take a quick break, to continue later with more clarity.

Once you have mapped out your book then it's time for the fun part. It's time to write. Let's look at what that's all about.

THREE

WRITE OUT

I'M NOT MUCH OF a baker but over the years I have given it a try a few times. It was a cold winter day a few years ago when I decided to bake some brownies to go along with a hot chocolate my kids and I decided to drink. I didn't have a brownie mix so I looked online for a scratch recipe and ran out to the store to grab the ingredients. I was meticulously planning as if for major surgery. I followed the recipe to the T, measuring, stirring, combining, and sifting. I wanted these brownies to be perfect. I greased the pan, poured in the mix, put it in the oven for forty-five minutes at 350 degrees. I set the timer on my phone and prepared for the production of my masterpiece. We were so excited! We couldn't wait. Forty-three minutes later we shot out of the bedroom, mouths watering. We opened the oven and to our surprise we saw a pan full of brownie batter. We had forgotten to start the oven! This situation reminded me of a very valuable concept. If you don't get started, all of the planning and preparation in the world means nothing.

What's true for brownies is also true for book writing. This chapter will describe the phase where we get started writing the book

The mantra I always work with is, "if you can think, you can write." The things we write come from how we think. Words don't suddenly appear out of nowhere. To get good content, all you need to do is sift through your thoughts, refine them, and write them out. Some people think writing involves having special or unique knowledge. This isn't entirely correct. You don't have to be the best on the topic you want to write about, as long as you are willing to put a substantial amount of time in research and writing.

Writing can be something that comes intuitively, but not everyone experiences this. The implication of this is that you don't have to necessarily write the chapters in successive order, chapter one doesn't have to be the first chapter that you will write, and you don't have to write chapters out in succession. It is important for you to flow with the inspiration that comes to you; if you are inspired to write chapter six first, then go for it, and continue to flow with your inspiration until you complete the whole book. For someone who has never written a book in the past, you may feel compelled to write the chapters in succession, even if don't have the right inspiration to write that particular chapter. The most important thing to determine the chapter you will write is where your creative intuition and inspiration lead you. As a writer, you are to surrender yourself to the leading of your inspiration.

> *"if you can think, you can write."*

But what if you don't feel 'inspired' to write a particular chapter first? What if you don't feel 'inspired' at all? Then, you have to rely on habit and discipline. Start a chapter and keep going until you finish it. Follow your outline. Maybe inspiration will come in the process. Maybe it will come tomorrow. But write, whether you feel inspired or not. The important thing is to write. Many people use a lack of inspiration as an excuse for why the book isn't written.

Without mincing words, writing your first draft is very intimidating. However, it is a bridge you must cross. The first draft will be messy, it will be rough, and it will not look anything like the book you want to write. The first draft is sometimes called the vomit draft or the rough draft, and it's not suitable for anyone to read. The purpose is for you to get all the words and thoughts out of your head and on paper. There is no editing in this phase. It isn't uncommon for people who are writing their first book to be fixated on making every word sound right, making sure that every punctuation is properly applied, etc., while making their first draft. Doing all these will distract you and waste your time – no one gets it right with their first draft, not even the most experienced, and talented writers. There will always be time to fine tune and edit the work to your taste, but first of all, you have to write. Again, this is the stage to allow your inspiration to flow, dominate and dictate. And if inspiration is fleeting, rely on habit and discipline to get you through.

Depending on the kind of book you are writing, you may want to include certain statistics, images, quotes or anything similar. For such things, you may need to take a break to research for what you need. When things like that come up, just continue your work. Don't break your line of thought or creative process to research, it may be difficult for you to get back into the flow once you break it. What you can do in this case is to simply make a note where the quote – or anything that you want to include – should be.

> *You can make it appear in italics and highlight it to remind yourself.*

Of course, there could be exceptions, the important thing is to always trust your creative instinct. For instance, if you want to include a story, and you have the right inspiration to write the story at that moment, you can draft the story as you write. However, anything that can take you to the internet should be avoided as much as possible. Your intentions may be to search for a quote on Google, you may end up finding yourself on YouTube watching videos of dancing babies – I kid you not. Trust the process and flow with it. Don't overthink anything during your first draft; make mistakes, commit blunders, laugh at your blunders, but by all means, keep writing. A lot of inexperienced writers will constantly beat themselves up over not getting the words right at the beginning. It is a complete waste of time to concentrate on such things while you are writing your first draft. The truth is that you are going to spend more time editing the work and making it readable than the time you will spend writing. Just get the words out first and work towards making it better at the editing stage.

While I have emphasized the importance of flowing with your inspiration, it is important for you to have your outline by your side as well. The whole purpose of creating an outline in the first place is to prevent you from veering off. It's very easy to get dragged to another topic entirely if you don't make the deliberate effort to stick to your outline. With your outline in hand, you can easily check for each section in your chapter and get back to writing.

CREATING THE TIME TO WRITE

Unless you have wealthy parents that you depend on for finances, you will definitely need to work, go to school, or be engaged in one activity or the other. Creating time to write may be very difficult. For many people, they have to go to work in the morning and come back in the evening, spend time with friends and family, etc. There are many important activities that consume a lot of our time, making it difficult to create the needed time to write. However, it is important for you to find a consistent time to write if you ever want to complete your book. It goes without saying that books don't write themselves, you have to write, one way or the other.

No matter how busy you may be, you have to create the time to write. When John Grisham started his writing career, he was

> *Just get the words out first and work towards making it better at the editing stage.*

a lawyer and a new dad, meaning that he was extremely busy. Still, he created time to write. He would get up an hour or two early to write a page every day. The trick is to develop a writing habit. Developing a writing habit will go a long way in helping you complete your first draft and it will also help you develop a lifelong creative habit that will always be useful. In the case of John Grisham, part of his writing habit involved getting up early to write a page per day. Creating a writing habit may be as simple as going to bed early and waking up early and spending the first 2 hours of the day writing your draft. Find a quiet place and write every day. If you maintain this habit for about a month, it becomes an integral part of you. For you to be more productive with the time you spend writing, it may be advisable for you to set a target word count for each day or week; it could be writing one thousand words per day or any target that will be comfortable for you to work with. You shouldn't be in a hurry to put a book out, so you don't have to set a big target, to begin with, just something you can work with to build momentum.

The writing process that works for each person may be different. It is important for you to stick with what works for you and be consistent with it. Writing inconsistently won't help you at all if you want to complete your book. Consistency and dedication are the key factors when it comes to completing your rough draft. One way to motivate yourself to complete the first draft is to promise yourself something you've always wanted. For instance, if you've always wanted to see a live basketball match or a concert, you can hinge your attendance of the next concert on your ability to complete your draft. If you are able to complete the draft within a particular period, then you're going to attend the next concert/basketball game. Staying motivated and inspired is very important in the creative process of any writer, you have to find ways to keep yourself motivate and inspired.

Here's another trick that will help you greatly, create a special space for yourself to write. It doesn't have to be fancy or truly special, it just has to be a different place from where you carry out your other activities. One of the reasons why you need to do this is to remove distraction and making it a place where the tools that can aid your writing are available. Maya Angelou rented a hotel room in her town when she needed to write. In addition, when you have a different space where you write, your brain becomes configured to the fact that once you step into that space, you are ready for getting serious work done. This space will be a constant reminder of your commitment to getting your book out. Again, it doesn't have to be a fancy space, it could be getting a table and chair in a different corner of your room.

GET FEEDBACK EARLY

One beginner mistake that a lot of writers that are just starting out make is to spend their entire time without every considering sharing the work with others to read. (Note: You are not sharing your rough draft with others. You are sharing perhaps your second or third draft, where your ideas are more refined, and your spelling/grammar errors are corrected.) It is one of the reasons why a lot of people never complete any book; they wait to finish the entire book before sharing it with anyone, just for them to hear that they may need to do a lot of rewriting because the book isn't as good as they thought. They become disappointed, completely lose interest, throw out the whole draft and forget about writing. This isn't unusual. Getting feedback for your work is very important. Knowing what someone else thinks about your work will help you know the direction to take your book, how to tweak it and make it more enjoyable for readers. This may sound contradictory to the idea of just writing without editing, but it isn't. Giving your work to people to read shouldn't alter your routine, you need to continue as you've always done; write without a break. However, don't make the mistake of not getting feedback for your work.

Don't just give your work to anyone to read, give it to someone who reads voraciously – someone you trust. The work of this person will not be to edit your work but offer an opinion on the "big picture." The "big picture" feedback is to give general opinions on things like clarity, quality of the work, etc. It is important to state that no matter how harsh their feedback may be, you should never get discouraged. Such comments are usually made to get the best out of you, not to discourage you. If the person isn't a professional editor, they may not know the best way to tell you that the book needs more work. If you're working with professionals, that will make the work very easy for you. If you don't have a voracious reader around you, whose opinion you trust, join a group of writers. They can be found in your community or on the internet. Your works-in-progress can be shared, and honest feedback given. If one writer's group isn't helpful, keep looking until you find the right fit.

FIGHTING WRITER'S BLOCK

Perhaps, you've never heard of writer's block, and you think it's a myth. I'm sorry to tell you that it isn't. Writer's block is a real struggle that writers face when they can't find the words to express themselves. I don't mean not finding the precise word to express a thought. I mean staring at a blank screen and having no idea of what to write about. They show up at their ordinary writing time, and no words, no thoughts, no inspiration, nothing. It's a very frustrating struggle to face, but it's real. For many writers, it can last for a long time and they find it difficult to recover from it. Facing a writer's block isn't about how gifted you are or how experienced you are, it happens to everyone. The strategy to deal with this could be different for each person, so you have to understand yourself and know what makes you feel inspired to write. Here are some tips that could work for anyone:

- If you are writing and you find yourself stuck or out of ideas, one way to tackle this is to take a break. Get up from your desk, forget everything about writing and concentrate on other things. The length of your break may vary, it may be for a few days, a week, etc. Just get up and forget you have a book to write for a while, you will come back energized and with fresh ideas.

- Reading a book could also work for you. In this case, you are taking a break as well, but you're taking a break to read other books to find inspiration. Writing can get boring, sometimes. Taking a break to read can help ease the boredom.

- Sometimes, the strategy is to just keep writing. This approach is what Maya Angelou used to do; she'd just write, even when she didn't feel the words coming as they should. She'd write the most random and boring things, but she'd keep writing anyway. Some people write, "I don't know what to write" over and over. Others might type out an article or story someone else has written, just to keep the writing going.

- Mark Twain believed that the secret for cracking writer's block is to break your complex tasks into small tasks that are manageable and then picking them one after the other. In other words, outline – which we've spoken about earlier.

- Sometimes, all you need to do is to stop when you are going well. This method was Ernest Hemingway's approach - to stop writing when you are good before you get to the stage where you'll be stuck. Pick up from where you left off the next day and repeat the same routine – make it your daily routine.

Overcoming your writer's block may require adopting a different approach, it may require you to start writing something else and use that to rediscover your inspiration. It may require traveling, it may require changing your writing routine or writing habit, etc. You may have to try different approaches before you find what really works for you.

There are times where the opposite of a writer's block happens, and you're overwhelmed with ideas. Take a minute or two and write down those ideas, then get back to your other trick is not to exhaust your resource, always keep some in your reserve.

- **Expert tip 1** – make sure you always track your daily word count; it'll help you get more serious with the task of getting your first draft out of the way. It is important for you to also track the number of times you spend on getting your word count daily. When you track your daily word count, you will be able to assess how long it would take to get to where you want to be.

    Always review your targets and your goals. Know how long you write, set milestones for yourself and reward yourself for reaching those milestones. If you're constantly unable to meet your milestones, review the things that are holding you back and try again.

- **Expert tip 2** – keeping a personal journal may be an interesting way to always track your progress, remind yourself of the reason why you started in the first place and the reason why you need to keep going. You can keep a journal for drafting your ideas too.

FOUR

ILLUSTRATE

I HAVE BEEN THE PASTOR of a church for almost 3 decades. It can be challenging to speak to the same audience over and over every week for years. As pastors we are called to teach principles and precepts. After years of speaking I have learned that principles and precepts are better understood when illustrations are used.

Illustrations can be examples, stories, props or even live performances. One of the best years we have ever had in ministry came as a result of a visual illustration. We asked our drama team to come up with several skits that represented people who needed to draw closer to God. The skits were performed with such skill that people's hearts were awakened. The drama team performed five to ten minutes skits on Sunday morning and the response was phenomenal. During a ten-month season, we had over 1500 people make commitments to draw closer to God. We had never seen such results before. I'm sure God helped in some of that but there was something about the illustrations that made the message clearer and the response greater. We think in pictures and when illustrations are used, we're actually using the language of the mind. Illustrations are essential to good writing.

Illustrations add beauty to your book because it involves making use of your creativity on a very different level. Illustration, in this case, does not only refer to the images you add but anything that adds color and beauty to the book.

When it comes to adding images, there are many ways to go about it. You will need to make a decision on the kind of images you want in the book, and your decision is going to be centered around the kind of book that you are writing. If you are writing a children's book, hand (or software) drawn illustrations are imperative. Children love images, and stock photos are of no use here. You will need to hire a professional illustrator who can help you bring your ideas to life. Depending on your budget, you can find different illustrators at a different price range. It's always advisable to go for the best; the impression that people get from your first book will last forever.

Illustrations add beauty to your book because it involves making use of your creativity on a very different level.

You can also use pictures that you took yourself, depending on the kind of book that it is, if your images are of high quality. Hiring a photographer whose style you like is important. Don't overlook photography students who may charge less in exchange for using the photographs in a portfolio. If you're writing a cookbook, you can attach your own pictures where appropriate, again, if they are of high quality. If you cannot take professional pictures, learn to do so, or hire someone. (As an aside, make sure you have professional photos of yourself. You need them for your book jacket, publicity stills, and media kit.) For some books, you can make do with stock images found online. Some stock images are free, but most charge a fee. Do not download random images off the internet and add it to your book without getting permission from the copyright owner first. That is illegal. Contact the copyright owner for permission. They may (or may not) charge a fee for permission. Some of the places you can get high quality images are

- Shutterstock
- Getty images
- Photogen
- istockphoto
- freeimages

One thing that always gives a lot of people a tough time is deciding the number of illustrations to include in the book. Although illustrations are good ways to add information and aesthetics to your book, don't overuse them. A traditional publisher will tell you the number of illustrations that you're expected to include in the book. If you're working alone, you'll need to determine the number of illustrations to include in the book. Unless you're writing a children's book, too many illustrations can distract the reader, and may even make them lose

To spice things up, you can create picture quotes that you can use in different places to emphasize some of your witty statements in the book.

interest. Your goal should be to keep the readers interested, but not to bore them.

Adding quotes to your book isn't as stressful as adding images. For quotes, you don't need to pay or get any special permission, as long as you include the name of the person to whom the quote is ascribed. There are many places to get quotes online, some of the most popular ones are

- BrainyQuote
- Wisdomquotes
- Quoteland Wikiquote

To spice things up, you can create picture quotes that you can use in different places to emphasize some of your witty statements in the book.

FIVE

TRANSITION

Something that doesn't get mentioned enough but is a key factor in how people enjoy reading a book is transition. The place of good transitions cannot be taken for granted for any reason. Transition deals with the flow of the work, how the previous chapter flows into the next, effortlessly. This element is most important in fiction and creative nonfiction, but it can make your book significantly better irrespective of your genre. In non-fiction genre books like self-help, motivational, spiritual, etc., each chapter can be dedicated to addressing different issues, creating a system where each chapter creatively flows into each other. However, imagine how readable and unputdownable it would be for the readers if you create a link between each chapter.

For fiction and creative nonfiction, making use of good transition is more-or-less compulsory. As a creative writer, you have the right to tell the story the best way you can, however, if that style bores the reader and makes them lose interest, you may have to reconsider. Readers like to be amused, they like suspense, and they love to read books that flow well. If readers have to reread sections repeatedly, then the flow is not as smooth as it should be. From scene to scene, and chapter to chapter, there should be a synchronization that brings the whole book together.

A good way to seamlessly transition from one chapter to the other is to give the reader a sense of what is to happen next; one chapter ending with a hint of what may come next. That way you don't only give yourself a good transition, you also create a bit of suspense – readers will be eager to know what happens next. One reason for having chapters in the first place is to give your readers a break and allow them to take soak in all that's happened in the chapter they've just completed; it's a sort of mental break before introducing more information.

> *A good way to seamlessly transition from one chapter to the other is to give the reader a sense of what is to happen next; one chapter ending with a hint of what may come next.*

The best way to start a chapter is with action, irrespective of genre. Action engages the reader and gets them excited about what's to come. If you're not writing a story, start with an action sentence, a sentence that will get them interested in the chapter. The level of the reader's excitement will drop if one chapter ends on a very high note, and the next chapter begins on a completely different level. Having a good transition and keeping the flow from chapter to chapter is a good way to keep the readers completely interested. For your book to have this element, you need to be very mindful and deliberate with how you open and close your chapters.

TRANSITION

Good transition doesn't mean that the next chapter has to continue where the previous chapter ends, it simply means you must be able to ease the readers in and create a connection. For instance, good flow in a nonfiction book would mean putting similar chapters side-by-side, thereby, creating a natural connection.

SECTION OFF

Chapters often benefit from using subtopics. In our earlier example about barbecue, the chapter about sauces can have subtopics for each type of sauce. Kansas City tomato-based sauce would be a subtopic, as would Alabama White (mayonnaise based) sauce and Carolina (with vinegar and/or mustard or tomato) based, style sauce, Texas style (which in itself contains many styles), Memphis (molasses based) sauce, Pittsburgh Red sauce, and dry rubs. If you are writing a book about different types of relationships, a chapter about same-sex relationships can have subtopics addressing male/male relationships, female/female relationships, relationships with people who don't ascribe to a particular gender, or transgenderism.

The best way to start a chapter is with action

There are different ways to create sections within a chapter. The first one, and the most obvious is to create a subtitle for each section to make the reader aware of what would be discussed in the next few paragraphs. Another way to create sections is to use creative words to open your paragraph and then introduce the subtopic to them. Words like, "Turning now to…", "So far this chapter has focused on __. The following paragraphs will discuss…" "Having discussed x in the previous paragraphs, I will now move on to…", etc. The most important thing is to create unity within the chapter, and the book as a whole. Creating sections in a book of fiction can be simpler, depending on what you're trying to achieve. The usual trick is to use:

****

One good thing with writing is that writers have a lot of creative freedom to try and invent new things. Don't be scared to try something new or to attempt something unusual in your transition. Everything you do as a writer must be deliberate.,

SIX

EDIT

I'M NOT KNOWN TO be the neatest person in the world when it comes to physical space. My personality is very spontaneous, and my environment reflects my persona. On the sixteen personalities test my personality is the Logician, typified by the absent-minded professor. That tells you a little bit about the way my mind works. My wife is extremely neat. She likes everything in its proper place all of the time. I have a special room at home I call my man cave. It's off limits to Kemi's upkeep. The house is hers, but my man cave is off limits. If I let her at it, I'm afraid I'll come home one day and there will be pink flowers all over the place! Since I maintain it, it is usually, well, creatively maintained. Whenever my wife Kemi complains about it, I just tell her I'm an abstract artist and my man cave is my canvas. A few months ago something came over me but I decided to clean up my "painting." I spent six hours cleaning out my man cave. I cleaned it from top to bottom removing all of the clutter. When I finished, I sat behind my squeaky-clean, black glass desk and looked at the detail of the room. I was stunned. There were things there that I had not seen in a long time. They were there but they were covered up in the clutter. Removing the clutter gave great clarity to my environment. I found myself spending more time in my man cave. There's something about order that is attractive to others and me. Kemi now likes to visit me in the cave—go figure. The same thing happens when you edit a book. Getting the clutter out draws you in and makes you want to camp for a while.

The joy of a writer doesn't always last for a long time. The happiness of completing a task births the struggle of starting another. A writer can be excited that they have completed their draft one minute, and suddenly, the fear of editing the book kicks in.

Let me break it to you, editing is hard work – maybe even harder than the writing itself. However, the moment after you complete your manuscript isn't the moment to plant fear into your heart, neither is it the moment for you to be worried about the next stage. The first thing you need to do is to congratulate yourself for completing a difficult phase that consumes a lot of wannabe writers. You did it! Be happy with yourself, rest, take yourself out, and enjoy the moment. Once you've been able to complete the first draft, I have no doubt that you'll be able to complete the whole book.

Now to the real task of editing. The first thing is to self-edit and make the manuscript better. At this stage you start paying attention to a lot of the things you ignored during the writing stage. I mentioned the need to take a break earlier; take a break and make it a long one. It's better to look at the manuscript with a fresh perspective when you start editing, and that can only happen when you've taken a break from thinking about the book for a while. I've been in situations where I would constantly omit a mistake, even after reading it several times. It happens because my mind is reading what I intended to write, not what I actually wrote. However, when you take a break, you can easily read and spot mistakes in your draft.

Once you self-edit your first draft, you can choose to continue self-editing, or hire an editor. While it's important for every writer to hire the service of a professional editor at some point in the editing process, I don't think it's a great idea to hire one too early, unless you are unsure of how to move forward.

One of the easy ways to edit is to listen to the manuscript. Play it using text to speech tools. During this process, your mistakes will become glaring. It's easier today because Microsoft Word has the option of 'Speak' which you can use to read out the text. Alternatively, both Mac and PC users can use the narrator option built into the system. Listening to your manuscript is a mind-blowing way to spot every little error and hear how the manuscript would read.

Editing forces you to look at the book as a whole.

In the editing process, there are many things to look for like organization, content and paragraph structure. A lot of people make the mistake of thinking that editing only involves correcting things like punctuation, grammar, and other writing errors, but all those are usually done while proofreading. Editing forces you to look at the book as a whole: Is it organized? Is the content presented with clarity? Is it in a logical order? While editing your manuscript, here are some things that will aid you:

Do away with subtle redundancies

There are many ways that writers use redundancies, and you should try to avoid them as much as possible. Unless you're writing a creative book and you're trying to use it as an effect, redundancies make the work boring to read. For instance, a sentence like, "He blinked his eyes" has subtle redundancy because if he isn't blinking his eyes, what else would he be blinking? Here's another one, "I nodded my head in agreement". The whole idea of nodding is to show agreement, and the only part of the body that can be nodded is the head. Redundant statements like that should be avoided in your final manuscript.

Show not tell

Readers want you to show them what's happening, not just for you to tell them. Showing will engage the readers' imagination, it will give them work to do, which readers tend to like a lot. When you show readers, they can easily draw their conclusions. In order words, don't spoon-feed readers, let them arrive at their conclusions.

Be more succinct

Even after you must have removed all the redundant words in the book, you have to look for ways to pass your message across with fewer words. The readers may easily lose interest if you constantly go for unnecessarily lengthy sentences. It's okay if you can't find any other alternative, but at each turn, ask yourself if there's a way you can pass your message across with fewer words.

Communicate, not impress

This is very common among young writers or those with little experience. They are always looking for ways to impress with their vocabulary and use of language. While it is wrong to go for simple words because you assume that they will not understand the big ones, it is also wrong to unnecessarily use difficult words simply because you want to impress them. The only place where you have the liberty to do as you want is poetry.

Your goal as a writer should always be to communicate your ideas in the most succinct and easy to understand words. People are paying to read your ideas; they are not paying to be impressed by your vocabulary. Your readers shouldn't have to read your book with a dictionary close by.

THE IMPORTANCE OF FEROCIOUS EDITING

Editing can be said to be the life of any piece of writing. If you want your book to be readable, you must make it error-free. Nobody wants to read a book and be constantly bombarded with errors, be they grammatical or typographical. Readers expect you to do the relentless work of thoroughly editing your book. While one or two unintentional errors can be excused, your aim should be

> *Your goal as a writer should always be to communicate your ideas in the most succinct and easy to understand words.*

to have a book that is completely error-free. The truth is that anyone can get anything published. With enough money, you are likely to find a vanity publisher who will publish anything you write without changing a word. Sometimes, the difference between a good writer and an average writer is the amount of time they pour into editing their work.

If you're planning to go through the traditional publishing channel, it's important that your work must be in its best form for you to ever get a chance of being considered. Traditional publishers will pay you an advance against royalties, and then they will pay the royalties on your sale. They're taking huge risks; risks they can't afford to take on poorly written manuscripts. No matter how creative you are with words, if your grammar is poor, and your punctuation is horrible, you are not likely going to get any publisher to accept your manuscript. Similarly, if your arrangement and organization are awful, you stand next to no chance with a publisher. Thoroughly self-editing your manuscript is a good way to separate yourself from the crowd. Many people are looking for the opportunity to get published and doing a thorough job of editing and proofreading your book will help you stand out. Once you finish editing, it's time to prepare for printing the book.

SEVEN

TYPESET

I LOVE WATCHING FOOT RACES. Perhaps I admire runners because I have never been a good one. I cycle for fitness, which I consider much easier. Runners have my respect. One aspect of racing that seemed to be contradictory was the way runners started their race—especially sprinters. We know they will be upright when they run, so why start in a low four-point position?

The runner starts in a crouched position with the front knee over and both hands on the starting line. The back knee is on the ground next to the front ankle. On the "set" both legs are extended so that the hips are slightly higher than the shoulders. The shoulders should lean slightly over the starting line. The front knee is bent about 90 degrees and the back knee about 110 to 130 degrees. The majority of the body weight is between the hands and front leg. On the "go," the runner pushes off with the legs and takes off.

This posture actually allows the runner to get to maximum speed quicker. The key to getting to top speed faster in a sprint is getting set. Without the structure of the set the results of the race would not be as desirable. In a similar manner the "set," typeset prepares the reader to take off running with your book in an organized fashion.

When you're already to this stage, you're already at the edge of completing the whole book production process. It's an important step, it determines how the text comes out in the final print.

Simply explained, typesetting is the process of setting text onto a page. This is a task that is usually done by the typesetter, and it involves carefully arranging the interior of the book, in order to give the reader a pleasant reading experience. I've picked up several books in the past, and even though they had good covers, the arrangement of the interior really turned me off. The formatting, the spacing, the alignment, everything was poorly done, and I had to force myself to look beyond all those and read the book. You wouldn't want readers to pick up your book and get turned off, even before reading a single word, would you? This is why typesetting is one of the most important aspects of book publishing, it has the ability to make or mar the whole work you've done.

Typesetting is the process of setting text onto a page.

The work of the typesetter involves determining the size of the margins and picking what would be the right font typeface and the style of the chapter headings.

Without mincing words, typesetting controls the readability of the book. When the readability of a book is poor, its commercial success will be greatly affected. Typesetting can be said to be a form of visual communication, one that shouldn't be overlooked under any circumstance.

HOW DOES TYPESETTING WORK?

Many unpublished writers have no idea what typesetting is or what it does. If you don't either, you are in good company. The reason why people barely know how typesetting works is that typesetting can be said to be successful when the readers are oblivious to it. Good typesetting, according to experts, isn't obvious. No one notices that the font fits the genre perfectly, no one comments on how perfect the trim size is, and no one lauds the typesetter or the writer for the perfect margins. However, when these things aren't perfect, the reader will know that there's something unpleasant about the book.

The typesetter looks out for things like a ladder of hyphenated words, double spacing between words, poor word spacing, etc. With how it's been described, it can seem like something you can quickly get done in Microsoft Word and move on, but that would be a grievous mistake. The best way to go is to either hire a typesetter or get it done yourself. If you choose to get it done yourself, there are many typesetting tools that you can use, but if you don't know what to look for, a professional is best. The kind of book that you've written will determine if you can go down the DIY route or if you'll need to hire a typesetter. A children's book with a lot of illustrations needs a specific visual look, and hiring a typesetter is the best option. If you've decided to hire a typesetter, it's important that you look at typesetters that work in your genre, and make sure you get familiar with their style.

> *Typesetting controls the readability of the book.*

EIGHT

PRINT

In this age of social media, people have carefully curated images. Everything posted has been rigorously lit, shot with the best camera available, staged with the best props and meticulously captioned. You created the best content ever, and the best captions. You post it, waiting for your likes and comments. THEN, you see the typo. Sometimes you can fix it. Sometimes you have to delete and repost. That is the print process, writ small.

At this stage, you should be pumped and happy. You have done the hard work, you have labored for many months, and right now, all that's left is for you to take your work to the printer and get those beautiful hard copies out. The printing process is like a woman going into labor after nine months of endurance and finally delivering a baby. For most women, seeing their baby for the first time makes all the pain worth it. The same thing happens to a writer.

However, it is not yet over. Printing is as important as any other aspect of the publishing process, and it's important for you to choose your printing options wisely. I have spoken extensively about the possibilities of both self-publishing and using traditional publishers.

Traditional publishers are the publishing firms who are set up to help writers handle everything about the book from editing to reaching the reader. For a writer fortunate enough to get a traditional publisher to buy the right to their book, all that's expected of them is to simply present a well-written manuscript, all other things would be handled by the publisher, including thorough editing and proofreading. Getting the attention of traditional publishers is hard work. They get a lot of pitches daily, so your work must be impressive. I explained the concept of sending proposals to traditional publishers earlier, you may revisit it to refresh your memory. Self-publishing is the direct opposite of traditional publishing, the writer handles everything from start to finish, including marketing and promoting the book.

Another alternative that many writers are going for now is independent publishing. A lot of people often confuse independent publishing and self-publishing, but they are not the same. Independent publishers can be defined as publishers that do not belong to a large conglomerate or multinational publishing house, such as HarperCollins or MacMillan. It is a much smaller publisher, with a special focus. What is important to know is that independent presses make up about half of the market share of the publishing industry. What a lot of authors now prefer to do is create an independent press, where they create own books, or imprints. In short, they create their own publishing house, however, on a small scale. All

Go for quality in your printing.

PRINT

the books you write will be published by your own publishing house, with every right belonging to you.

A subset of the independent press is a vanity press. A vanity press will publish any manuscript. You pay all the fees for them to publish the book. It is something to be wary of, especially if you don't have a great deal of money to throw around. If you're simply looking at publishing a book as a gift for someone you love or something similar, then a vanity press may be a good fit for you.

I feel the urge to emphasize the importance of editing once again. Edit. Edit. Edit. Then hire an editor to catch what you miss. Go for quality in your printing. Get quality paper.

NINE

HOW TO MARKET YOUR BOOK

One of the most successful financial books ever written is *Rich Dad Poor Dad* by Robert Kiyosaki and Sharon Lechter. To date it has sold over 32 million copies. In the book Kiyosaki tout's advice given to him by his dad and his best friend's dad. His dad, a middle-class working man, and his friend's dad—the rich guy—was an entrepreneur. One of the points he stressed in the book is the importance of marketing for success. He said, "The most important specialized skills are sales and marketing. The ability to sell—to communicate to another human being, be it a customer, employee, boss, spouse, or child—is the base skill of personal success[1]

The fact that you've written a very good book doesn't mean it's going to sell. Books don't sell themselves. For a book to be commercially successful, it doesn't have to be the best book written, it simply has to have the best marketing strategy. The popular

---

[1] Kiyosaki, Robert and Lechter, Sharon, Rich Dad Poor Dad, Warner Books, New York, 2000. (kindle edition, page 191.)

authors with bestsellers that you know today didn't become successful solely because of their talent. A lot of planning goes into marketing the books as well. Whether you're planning to self-publish or you have a traditional publisher, marketing your book is essential.

If you're writing your first book, you cannot escape marketing your book. No one knows you as a writer, no one is anticipating your book, and you certainly don't have interviews lined up for you. It is therefore critical for you to put the book in people's hands and make them aware of it. Selling your books is like any other business out there. You need to make people aware of the existence of the product, and why they need it. Your family and friends are probably going to buy your book, but I'm sure you didn't write your book just for it to be sold to your family and friends alone.

Social media and the change in how people interact with media has altered the face of marketing generally, and book marketing specifically. If you have a large social media following, those followers can be converted to book buyers. In the past, print and television media used to be the marketing gatekeepers. Now, social media has taken over in many areas. However, in order to appeal to the broadest audience possible, no stone should be left unturned in the process of marketing the book. The type of readers you're trying to target will determine the best medium for marketing your book. If you're working with a traditional

> *For a book to be commercially successful, it doesn't have to be the best book written, it simply has to have the best marketing strategy.*

publisher, chances are that they will handle everything around the marketing of your book, therefore, the strategies to be discussed here will focus on self-published writers.

The most important thing a self-published author should know is that marketing is hard work – it takes planning, organization, and consistent action. However, the good thing about a good marketing plan is that it makes the work easier for your subsequent publications, it can help to build a fan base. I know that another layer of work may not seem appealing after the enormous time and effort you've put into the process of completing the book, but this layer of work determines if you'll become a multiple New York Times bestselling author or if this is the only book you'll ever write. Marketing is critical if you want to hear people talk about your book.

> *If you're writing your first book, you cannot escape marketing your book.*

I. SOCIAL MEDIA

Social media has risen to become one of the most effective ways of marketing in the 21st century. Using social media is even more important if your target audience is young readers. There are billions of users across all social media platforms, the opportunities are huge. Social media users spend a lot of time scrolling through their timeline, and you can easily target them with the right ad.

There are many opportunities for marketing on social media, and some of them are absolutely free. For instance, a platform like Facebook allows for the creation of groups which like-minded can join. As a result, there are many writers' groups on Facebook. You can join the groups that are most appropriate to your genre, and market your book in these various groups. Similarly, all social media platforms allow the use of targeted ads, and you can easily create ads that target the kind of people you want to sell your book to. Another way to get your book to new audiences is to work with influencers in the book niche. It may involve giving them a free copy to read and paying them to write about your book to their audience. It is an effective way to get people to know about your book.

Beyond all the social media marketing tips that I have shared above, you can also do a lot of promotion on your own page, (assuming you are on Instagram, Facebook, Twitter, or some other platform that appeals to you.) using it to increase your followers and to sell your book. You need to know, however, that you are not going to increase your followers or sell your book by just posting images of your book on your page, you will have to make a lot of deliberate and calculated moves. Different social media platforms require different approaches, I will work you through how to successfully use social media to market your book:

Use great images

One thing that cannot be emphasized enough for any social media related marketing is the use of great visuals. It's important to be able to catch the attention of people with well-designed high-quality images, that's the only reason they'd scroll back to read what you've written, and it's the reason they'd click on your profile. Great images are very important for any social media platform you may be targeting. While you can't escape posting images on Instagram, Twitter and Facebook are very different. However, posts with images get more engagement than ordinary posts.

One of the things you have to pay attention to here is your book cover. We haven't talked about this at all, however, it's very important. The very first thing that will catch your eye about a book sitting in a bookshop is the cover, and then the title. A good cover makes people curious and interested in reading a book. You have to put a lot of thoughts and planning into creating a good book cover, and you should endeavor to hire the best designers to help with it. The kind of cover you create for your book can affect the commercial success you're going to get. In creating a book cover, go for something that will make the reader curious, something that draws them in but doesn't give away anything from the book.

Post good images of yourself holding the book and of others holding it. Create aesthetically pleasing pictures using different props, and get graphic designers to create different looks for the book title. When you hold book signings or readings, post good images of these events, with good captions attached. Identify quotes and punchlines from the book and create images for them. People like to see short catchy lines; it'll make them more curious about the book.

Use appropriate hashtags

Hashtags have become integral to getting more people to see and engage with content. Normally, the only people who would see your posts on their social media timelines are those who follow you; others simply have to rely on stumbling on your page or someone sharing/retweeting your post. However, when you use hashtags appropriately, more people get to see your content. For instance, if you use a hashtag like #bookstagram, anyone that follows that hashtag will get to see your content until the time that newer posts overshadow yours. Similarly, when topics related to your niche are trending, you can use the corresponding hashtag. For instance, if it's #worldbookday, you can simply make use of the hashtag and talk about your book.

Engage with followers

Engaging with your followers is an effective way to build loyalty and friendship with them. Don't just post and leave, respond to your followers and like their comments. While creating content, invite others to share their opinion and ask questions. People share content every minute, and older posts get moved to the bottom when newer ones are created. The more engagement your contents get, the more likely is it to remain at the top. Don't be afraid to ask questions or start a conversation. For instance, if you're a fiction writer, you can ask your followers to talk about their favorite characters, their reading habits or genre pet peeves. Schedule Q & A's with your followers for a more personal touch, letting them get to know a bit about you.

It's also good to get engaged with the life of your followers, liking their posts or comments, congratulating them when they do something amazing, and showing them that you care. A lot of big brands with millions of followers are always seen engaging their followers, so you have no excuse whatsoever.

Run campaigns and contests

Campaigns and contests have become very popular on social media, and they are one of the ways to increase the popularity of your book and your brand. This may not sound very appealing to a lot of people because it involves giving something away for free, it could be a signed copy of the book, a ticket to your book signing, etc. It's a very effective way to build a brand. If you're looking at marketing your book solely from the perspective of selling your book, then you're doing it wrong. Book giveaways are also a way to identify loyal and dedicated followers that will be interested in buying any book you write. Therefore, your attention shouldn't just be on the immediate gain, but on using it to build your career.

2. CREATE A WEBSITE

Creating a personal website is very important for any published author, and it's not something you can negotiate if you're trying to effectively market your book. People will definitely want to know more about you, they want to know about upcoming events, and the place they can go to for all this information is your website. Your website is part of your unique brand, a brand that makes a lot of people interested in your personality. The things that you have on your author's website are:

- Your bio

- Your email address (or ways to contact you social media)
- Your photo
- Excerpts from your book
- Link to buy your book

3. BUILD AN EMAIL LIST

This tactic is something essential that must be added to your writer's website. After you've been able to get people to show interest in your writing and visit your website, it's not likely that they will come back from time to time to check for updates. The best thing to do is to create newsletter signup where you can send them frequent updates. Through that list, you can easily keep in touch with people that have shown interest in you. It is a good way to secure the sales of your books – even the ones you haven't published yet. It's very easy to turn your subscribers into paying customers.

It's important that you send only relevant emails, and don't overuse it. A monthly email update is a very effective way of staying fresh in the mind of your subscribers. Email marketing is a long-term strategy, take it slow and use it to build a solid base for yourself.

4. USE BOOK REVIEWERS

Even though the literary world has changed a lot over the years, traditional book reviews are still one of the most trusted ways to bring attention to a new book. The more reviews your book gets, the more popular it becomes. Reach out to book reviewers in your genre and convince them to read your book and write something about it. This tactic is similar to the idea of reaching out to social media influencers in your genre which I mentioned earlier. Amazon reviews are also very important, the more reviews you get, the better.

CONCLUSION

BOOK WRITING IS NOT an easy task. A lot of people come to writing with the mindset of just writing and getting the book published, making quick and easy money. I'm sorry to break it to you that the only quick and easy money you'll make is that of your family and friends who have no choice but to support you. Excellence and hard work are very important in writing, they cannot be jettisoned. In many societies, being a writer comes with many responsibilities. A writer is expected to be intelligent and have a good understanding of the language in which they choose to write. These are the minimum things that are as expected of a writer. You can't afford to have a book that is poorly written or lacks basic organization.

There are many books out there, and readers have many options. They take their time to consider why they should invest their money and time in your book. The decision becomes very easy if your title is uninspiring, the book cover is poor, they flip through and the typesetting is bad, they read a few sentences and there are errors, etc. As a writer, it's important for you to respect your readers. To respect them is to invest a lot of quality time and effort into writing and publishing your book. To put a poorly written book in front of your readers is to disrespect them.

Starting to write a book for the first time may seem like a daunting task, but all that's needed is for you to take that first step. You're not going to finish your book by magic, you'll have to work hard. However, the best way to shatter your fear is to start, anyway. I have explained how you can start and finish your book, but one thing I haven't mentioned is how easy it is for people to give up before writing a single word. As long as you have something to share with the world, just start writing. It's easy to be frustrated because you are not getting the right punchline to write in the first sentence, but just write something anyway, anything. If after completing the first draft, the book isn't still good enough, you can destroy it and forget that you ever wrote that draft. However, you'd have overcome your fear, and you'd be able to work on other ideas without the regret of what could have been.

With the tips that I've shared with you in this book, I am confident that you're only a few steps away from having your own printed book in your hands. Go off now, get to work…